Stan Starsky Snacks

The gluten free, dairy free, no processed sugar healthy snacks
cookbook to look and feel fantastic

by Stan Starsky

Big Universe Publishing

Published by Big Universe Publishing
www.biguniversepublishing

ISBN: 978-0-9856540-1-6

Dedication

I would like to dedicate this book to everyone who has bought this book.
(That means you—thanks!)

Endorsements

"I proudly and publicly declare that this might be the best snack book ever written. I absolutely love this cookbook. I will shamelessly and proudly promote this book everywhere." *—Anonymous*

Disclaimer

Don't put anything into your mouth until you talk to a doctor.

Statements in this book have not been approved by the FDA, meaning information has not been evaluated by the Food and Drug Administration. Nothing should be interpreted as an attempt to offer a medical opinion. The writer{s} or publisher{s} of this book are not responsible for any adverse reactions, effects, or consequences resulting from the use of any recipes or suggestions herein or procedures undertaken hereafter. If you have questions about food, diet, nutrition or holistic health, please do your own research and consult with your care practitioner. If you are pregnant, nursing, have a medical condition or are taking any medications, please consult your health care practitioner before making any changes to your diet.

Table of Contents

Forward

Hi! My name is Stan Starsky, and I don't claim to know much about anything except for one thing—SNACK FOOD.

Imagine that you call me for advice:

You: What is the best time of year to hang glide?

Stan Starsky: I really don't know.

You try another question:

You: My pet rock seems distant and emotionally unavailable, what should I do?

Stan Starsky: I don't know, some geologists do couples counseling.

And again:

You: What should I put in my terrarium?

Stan Starsky: I am not sure. Maybe some grass clippings and a frog.

And for some reason, you keep asking:

You: Stan, please tell me how to make super-wholesome, no-processed sugar, mouth-watering delicious snacks.

Stan Starsky: Finally, a question I can answer! You have come to the right place. Please read on and prepare to embark on an exciting snack food journey.

A Socratic look at junk food. You know that junk food is so tempting to eat. The ads are upbeat and entertaining; it's cheap and convenient, and the snacks come in all sorts of interesting colors.

But take a second to think about a few things:

- Will artificial flavors and colors make you more attractive and vital?
- Will chemical additives give you clean-burning, long-lasting energy?
- Will artificial sweeteners, emulsifiers, fillers, preservatives, stabilizers and caking agents improve your health?
- Do artificial preservatives, and processed sugars fight off disease?
- Does anybody actually like rhetorical questions?

Of course not! There's a reason it's called junk food. You wouldn't fuel your car with junk gas, so why would you fuel your body with junk food?

What if you could find a way to eat wholesome snacks that taste just as good as all of the junk out there? If someone could make that happen, that would be a game changer. You could improve your health, appearance, and vitality, all while eating delicious snacks.

Fortunately for you, I have been working on just that type of project for a very long time, it is practically my life mission, and now I am ready to let you in on my secrets.

The History of Stan Starsky

Like you, I also have a past. We actually have a lot in common. We both have a past.

It all started many years ago when I operated a vending machine route. I started small, distributing snacks from a minivan. Then, as my route expanded, I moved up to a cargo van. Eventually, I was driving around in a fourteen-foot box truck delivering salty chips, candies, and soda. My business grew over the five years that I spent as a junk food dealer.

So how did I wind up writing a wholesome cookbook? Hold on. I'm getting there.

I can't say how I justified my years as a distributor of junk. Maybe it was the thrill of the cash business or the glamor of driving a loud ten-year-old cramped box truck with a broken air conditioner in the height of the summer. Whatever the reason, I had essentially become a fallen snack angel—an empty soul delivering empty calories.

I have to admit, running a vending route is really great exercise. I was loading cases and cases of sodas and snacks on and off a truck into buildings all day long, burning lots of calories.

As a result, I would get really hungry. And after a while, I would stand in the back of the truck as my stomach rumbled, surrounded by food, but there was nothing I wanted to eat.

You see, when I first started the route, I would open some of the packages and eat the contents; the snacks sure tasted good, but I never felt too well afterward.

I was in a pretty dark place, *snackfully* speaking. I prefer not to talk about it. But I will anyway. I was overwhelmed and full of despair. My heart was heavy with memories of artificial flavors and preservatives. Imagine the scariest Edgar Allen Poe poem multiplied a million times then stuck inside a black hole—I am trying to say I was in a dark place.

I had to make a change—I wanted out of this snack enigma. (I don't know what enigma means, this word is kind of a mystery to me).

Maybe it was because I felt threatened by the candies, deep-fried chips, and other empty calories surrounding me. Or maybe I felt a bit guilty for peddling barren calories and needed to even up my snack food karma. Or maybe I just liked the irony of it.

In any event, I embarked on a snack food vision quest. I became obsessed with making healthy, exciting snack foods out of all those usually boring fruits, vegetables, and nuts that everyone knows they should eat, but no one *wants* to eat. And so, my quest began.

We are all told about the great benefits of eating fruits, vegetables, and nuts.

- More (and more consistent) energy throughout the day
- A healthy glow
- Longer life
- An improved immune system
- Better mental alertness
- X-ray vision

Conventional wisdom says that the only healthy alternative to a truck full of junk food is to eat some fruits, nuts, etc. But eating bananas, apples, and fruit sometimes gets a little boring. I love eating fruit. However, it is hard to maintain a long-term committed snack relationship with pretty dull food. Imagine marrying a banana.

I tried buying store-bought granola bars because I was somewhat of a high adrenaline-loving, live life on the edge, thrill-seeking-maniac. Most of those granola bars contain an outrageous amount of sugar, so I began formulating my own granola recipes. My early attempts were discouraging. I could not get the granola bars to stick together and form a bar.

Soon I began to despair. I was unable to envision a way out of this downward snack spiral. My emotional frame of mind took me back to that overly dramatic dark poetry wrapped in a black hole headspace. Darkness descended on my soul, and I was unsure if I could muster the courage to carry on.

But I went there. I don't know how I found the strength.

I was pushing and going deeper than I ever thought I could go, and one day, suddenly, I had a granola breakthrough. It was cathartic. The sun seemed shinier, the grass was greener, music filled the air, and delicious, wholesome snacks came into being in my kitchen.

After a few more revolutionary snack breakthroughs, I knew I had to keep going. Soon, one discovery led to another. With snack momentum on my side, I kept testing and testing, spending hundreds of hours in the kitchen, until finally, it all came together.

A friend of mine said, "you are like Beethoven." I asked him what he meant by that, and he did not know—so that ended that conversation. He meant that we all have a little genius, and I would like to think I focused mine on snack food. And now, after years of toiling in anonymity, I am ready to share my snack superpowers with you.

It is true. I did own a vending business, and it was called Olympic City Vending. I also spent a lot of time inventing new granola recipes.

Control Your Snack Food Destiny

This book is a snack anthem for the snack downtrodden. The recipes I have created are designed to take away the pain of preservatives, processed sugar, gluten, emulsifiers, and other food additives.

When you make snacks from scratch, you take back control of your life, even in a small way. You can't control the chemicals that manufacturers put into junk food, but you can control the wholesome ingredients of the snacks you create.

Start by setting some achievable snack goals, but don't be afraid to stretch yourself a little – this is where the snack magic happens. Always keep in mind the snack paradox: "When you are eating this, you are not eating something else."

A snacronym (pronounced snack-cronym) to help you with your Snack Goals:

S—Set a goal to eat a little better

N—Not too big—just a small goal

A—A is for "apple," and like most ancient mystical wisdom, it is a metaphor. In this case, the apple represents all fruits and is also a specific fruit. Chew on that, and by chew on that, I mean eat the snacks but also think about it deeply. There is so much subtext in this book.

C—Can I do this? Yes, you *can* do this.

K—I don't know many words that start with K. Actually, "know" does. Now you know another useless acronym.

I am sure you found the above exercise extremely helpful, so now that you have set some goals, let's move on.

I've included detailed instructions for each recipe, but you don't need to follow them closely to get great results. For example, if the recipe calls for 1/8 cup of something, just throw in a small handful. Where it says 1/4 cup, throw in a big handful. It's just snack food, so don't worry about it.

Recipes

Fruit and Nut Fun Bowl

Let me introduce the concept of a Fruit and Nut Fun Bowl. I invented the fun bowl more than twenty years ago because, as much as I like eating, say, an apple, sometimes the solo approach to fruit-eating is a little dull.

'Fun Bowl' sounds pretty ridiculous. A guy once scoffed at the name and said he thought it was unsophisticated and silly. So, he checked his **Yahoo** mail and used **Google** to find **blogs**. Apparently, people like silly names.

I have provided recipes for several of my favorite fun bowls, but there are infinite combinations. Eventually, you will come up with your favorites. I like my fun bowl on the chunky side but feel free to process yours as you like. When processing any fun bowl, stop every once in a while to test the consistency.

Cleaning tip

If you don't feel like cleaning the food processor right away, at least quickly rinse it with cold water. This will make it less sticky.

Fruit and Nut Fun Bowl—The Original

You might call this the bread-and-butter fun bowl or a comfort food fun bowl. If you don't have pecans, throw in a few more almonds. I eat this for breakfast and sometimes for lunch.

1/4 cup almonds	1 orange
1/4 cup pecans	1 apple
4 or 5 dates	1 banana

Process the nuts in a food processor for about ten seconds; then add the rest of the ingredients and process until chunky.

You can eat the fun bowl or decorate it by arranging apple or banana slices on top with a few additional almonds.

If you have ever purchased an acai bowl from a health food store, you may have other ideas for toppings, such as coconut, goji berries, chia seeds, etc. You don't have to decorate with toppings; either way is fine. Relax and enjoy.

Strawberry Fruit and Nut Fun Bowl

I like this fun bowl really chunky, so I tend to under-process it, but you should do yours your way. I can't help you with everything.

1/4 cup almonds	1 orange
1/4 cup pecans	1 apple
4 or 5 dates	1 1/2 cups strawberries

Add all the ingredients except the strawberries to a food processor and process for about ten seconds. Then add the strawberries and process the mixture for another ten or fifteen seconds.

Psychic mind reading: You think this is similar to the last recipe except that it has strawberries. Pick your own metaphor for the strawberries. One small thing can change everything.

You can eat the fun bowl or decorate it by arranging apple or banana slices on top with a few additional almonds.

If you have ever purchased an acai bowl from a health food store, you may have other ideas for toppings, such as coconut, goji berries, chia seeds, etc. You don't have to decorate with toppings; either way is fine. Relax and enjoy.

Fruit and Nut Fun Bowl—PG-13 Citrus Delight

Caution: Not for the young or faint of heart. This fun bowl has a strong adult flavor. This is a PG-13 fun bowl; a mature palate is required.

1 lime	1 orange
1 apple	1 teaspoon of honey
2 cups strawberries	2 cups strawberries
1/4 cup of pecans (about a handful)	

Put nuts and apple in a food processor and blend for about ten seconds. Squeeze the lime and then add the rest of the ingredients. Process for about ten more seconds.

You can eat the fun bowl or decorate it by arranging apple or banana slices on top with a few additional almonds.

If you have ever purchased an acai bowl from a health food store, you may have other ideas for toppings, such as coconut, goji berries, chia seeds, etc. You don't have to decorate with toppings; either way is fine. Relax and enjoy.

Fruit and Nut Fun Bowl—Sunrise

It is not just for breakfast anymore.

1 banana	1/4 cup of almonds or handful
1 to 2 cups pineapple	1/4 cup of pecans or handful
2 or more dates	apple (option)

Add nuts first and process for ten seconds. Add the rest of the ingredients and process.

A great way to wake up. But feel free to eat it anytime.

It is not just for breakfast anymore. I hear that saying a lot as well.

You can eat the fun bowl or decorate it by arranging apple or banana slices on top with a few additional almonds.

If you have ever purchased an acai bowl from a health food store, you may have other ideas for toppings, such as coconut, goji berries, chia seeds, etc. You don't have to decorate with toppings; either way is fine. Relax and enjoy.

Fun Bowl that does not have a name—"no fun" for short

Don't count out this fruit and nut bowl because it does not have a name. Keep in mind that it gets a little weird when you are serving this at a party or a trade show, and somebody says, "Hey, everybody who wants a No Fun, Fun Bowl.

2 apples	4 or 5 dates
1/4 cup walnuts	splash of orange juice (1/8 of a cup)
4 baby carrots	

Add carrots first and process. Then add the rest of the ingredients and process for about ten seconds.

Feel free to substitute almonds or pecans for the walnuts

You can eat the fun bowl or decorate it by arranging apple or banana slices on top with a few additional almonds.

If you have ever purchased an acai bowl from a health food store, you may have other ideas for toppings, such as coconut, goji berries, chia seeds, etc. You don't have to decorate with toppings; either way is fine. Relax and enjoy.

Fruit and Nut Bowl—Cantaloupe, so stay in town and get married

Very Important: I like most Fun Bowls to be chunky, but this is one I like really well blended.

Also, keep in mind that ginger is a wild card. There is no telling how strong the ginger will be, so proceed with fearless caution.

1/ 2 cantaloupe	1/4 cup of pecans
1/2 teaspoon spoon blended ginger	banana—optional
1/4 cup of almonds	apple

Put everything in the food processor. Pulverize

Eat

I know you can do it.

You can eat the fun bowl or decorate it by arranging apple or banana slices on top with a few additional almonds.

If you have ever purchased an acai bowl from a health food store, you may have other ideas for toppings, such as coconut, goji berries, chia seeds, etc. You don't have to decorate with toppings; either way is fine. Relax and enjoy.

Fun Bowl—called Banadate Alpecan (named after the ingredients)

Interesting Naming Fun Bowl Fact: The name of this one is Banadate Alpecan, and it is practically the whole recipe. I stole that concept from a soup called "Cream of Mushroom Soup." It really got me thinking. The people that name soup are super smart. The name gives you hints about what is in it. And now a fun bowl utilizes this logic as well—Banadate Alpecan Fun Bowl

So, all you have to do is remember the name, and you are home free.

1 banana	1/4 cup of pecans
3 or 4 dates	optional—coconut flakes
1/4 cup almonds	apple

Add nuts first and process for about ten seconds. Add the rest of the ingredients and process.

You can eat the fun bowl or decorate it by arranging apple or banana slices on top with a few additional almonds.

If you have ever purchased an acai bowl from a health food store, you may have other ideas for toppings, such as coconut, goji berries, chia seeds, etc. You don't have to decorate with toppings; either way is fine. Relax and enjoy.

I feel like I Am On Vacation—Fun Bowl

This will put you in vacation mode. Imagine that the food processor is like a time machine, but instead of taking you to a different time, it takes you to a different place. It is like a place machine, and we already have those.

1 banana	1/4 cup of almonds
1-2 cups of pineapple	1/4 cup of pecans
2 dates	apple (option)

Put nuts and banana in the food processor first and chop for a few seconds. Add the rest of the ingredients and process.

You can eat the fun bowl or decorate it by arranging apple or banana slices on top with a few additional almonds.

If you have ever purchased an acai bowl from a health food store, you may have other ideas for toppings, such as coconut, goji berries, chia seeds, etc. You don't have to decorate with toppings; either way is fine. Relax and enjoy.

I Still Feel Like I Am On Vacation—Fun Bowl

Remember to go for chunky. When serving this at your next company picnic or garage sale, you will probably hear, "Hey, give me seconds of ' Still Feel Like I Am On Vacation Fun Bowl.'" Feel free to quote me on that.

1 cup of strawberries	1/4 cup of pecans
1 cup of pineapple	1/4 cup of almonds
apple (option)	

Put nuts and banana in the food processor first and chop for a few seconds. Add dates and pineapple and process some more.

You can eat the fun bowl or decorate it by arranging apple or banana slices on top with a few additional almonds.

If you have ever purchased an acai bowl from a health food store, you may have other ideas for toppings, such as coconut, goji berries, chia seeds, etc. You don't have to decorate with toppings; either way is fine. Relax and enjoy.

Copycat Cashew Fun Bowl

Cashews instead of almonds or pecans can change everything.

1 cup of strawberries

1 cup of pineapple

apple (option)

3 or 4 dates

1/2 cup of cashews

Put nuts in the food processor first and chop for a few seconds. Add everything else and process some more.

You can eat the fun bowl or decorate it by arranging apple or banana slices on top with a few additional almonds.

If you have ever purchased an acai bowl from a health food store, you may have other ideas for toppings, such as coconut, goji berries, chia seeds, etc. You don't have to decorate with toppings; either way is fine. Relax and enjoy.

Some final Fruit and Not Fun Bowl thoughts

You can add a little ginger to any of the combinations. However, if you add ginger, add already blended ginger, or try and blend it down first.

You can add a little spinach to any fun bowl combination. It won't affect the taste but will add a few additional vitamins.

This ends the Fun Bowl section of the cookbook.

You are just beginning your snack food journey; you will soon discover a few dips, desserts, and granola recipes.

Hot Tomato Avocado Dip

Hot tomato Q and A

Question: What size chunks should everything be?

Answer: That is personal preference, but I think the garlic should be chopped up as small as possible, and the onion should be chopped into small pebble-sized pieces; the tomato pieces should still be chopped pea-sized but don't worry if the chunks are not round.

Question: I am thinking of a number between one and four; what number am I thinking of?

Answer: Four

1 tomato	1 clove of garlic
1/4 of an onion	pepper to taste
2 stalks of fresh basil (like half a pack)	a pinch of salt
3 tablespoons of olive oil,	

Chop garlic and onion into small pieces, put olive oil in a pan on low heat, and simmer for about 2 minutes.

Take the leaves off two large stalks of fresh basil (you can buy fresh basil in the produce section). Chop up the basil and chop up the tomato. Add the chopped tomato and basil to the pan and simmer on low heat for about 8 minutes. Mash the avocado into a paste and add it to the pan.
Stir everything until it is hot (about 2 or 3 more minutes).

Stir in a pinch of salt and some pepper.

I dare you to explain this recipe to someone without using the word "chop."

3 Dips and I am in love

On the first dip, I thought this is nice and it has potential, but the feelings were more platonic. I developed very strong feelings on the second dip and found myself smiling when thinking about it. On the third dip, everything changed.

1/2 apple	1/2 teaspoon sea salt
16-ounce bag of spinach	4 shakes of pepper
1 avocado	1 clove garlic
2 small spoonfuls of apple cider vinegar	

Peel the apple half. Put apple, spinach, apple cider vinegar, avocado, and garlic in the food. Process everything until it is a smooth dip.

Open your heart and mouth to this dip.

Onion Dip

1 large, sweet onion	1 cup coconut yogurt
1 garlic clove	2 tablespoons of olive oil
1/8 teaspoon sea salt – then salt to taste	

Food process onion and garlic until it becomes a paste-like consistency.
Put onion mix and olive oil in a large frying pan and heat at medium-low heat (on my stove 4 out of 10). Let it initially sit for a while, then stir as needed. Once it starts to caramelize, it will go pretty quickly.

Once the onion is caramelized, add it to the coconut yogurt and stir, then stir in the salt. Put this in the refrigerator for several hours. It takes a while for the flavors to come out.

**You can brown the onion without any oil, but it takes longer and is more work. Simply place pulverized onion in the pan and let it sit for a while (water will evaporate), then stir and continuously remove caramelized onion from the pan.

Guacamole

Another snack confessional. I know; I did not invent guacamole. Sometimes I just eat this with a spoon and not even worry about the chips. But this is how I eat it, and I hope you like it.

1 or 2 avocados

¼ sweet onion

1/2 lime, squeezed

1 small tomato about the size of a plum

Pepper to taste

2 or 3 shakes of cayenne pepper

2 dashes salt

Mash up avocado. Dice the sweet onion into small pieces and dice up the tomato into chunks. Mix avocado, onion, and tomato, and squeeze in the lime. Stir in sea salt, pepper, and cayenne pepper.

Avocado Dill Cucumber

I plead the fifth—no extra comments

1/2 avocado	1/2 small spoonful dill
Dash of sea salt	1/4 small spoonful lime
1/2 cucumber (peeled or unpeeled)	

Place all ingredients in a food processor and blend for about 45 seconds to a minute.

Add more sea salt if necessary. Result: Pretty Good.

Tomato Balsamic Vinegar

While I love onion and garlic, I recommend trying this mix one time without the onion or garlic—you might like it better that way. Another variation is to blend in an avocado with a dash of Tabasco, and you have Sloppy Guacamole. Great dip, but sometimes I eat it like a bowl of cold soup.

2 medium-sized tomatoes	2 to 3 tablespoons olive oil
1 garlic clove	16 big fresh basil leaves
dash of pepper to taste	4 tablespoons balsamic vinegar
1 small, sweet onion or 1/4 large, sweet onion	dash of sea salt to taste

Take all these ingredients and chop them up manually; then mix them in a bowl.

Or put garlic clove and onion in a food processor and process first. Add the rest of the ingredients and process some more. But keep it chunky like salsa.

Avocado Vanilla Dip

This makes a pretty good fruit dip.

1 avocado	1 tablespoon honey
1/4 teaspoon vanilla	1/2 cup coconut milk

Thoroughly mash the avocado in a bowl. Mix in the coconut milk. Mix in the vanilla and honey.

Avocado Vanilla Dip is a dish better served cold. So let it sit in the refrigerator for a while before eating.

The Granola Code

An Open Letter to My Fellow Granola Connoisseurs

For me, granola is not granola—it's the poster snack of wholesome foods. That's why I became obsessed with it. I have experimented with hundreds of subtle variations. The variations were so subtle that nobody could tell them apart.

So, I pared down my granola list, but some still say I have too many varieties. For that reason, I recommend a sequence for trying the granola recipes. You'll find that sequence below.

I hope you will develop your own versions as you hone your granola skills. May the student become the master.
Good luck, and enjoy the granola.

Granola's Main Components

- Sweeteners

- spices

- fillers

- process

Some Thoughts on Sweeteners

Although I have tried honey, maple syrup, and blue agave, I mostly use honey and maple syrup. I find that honey and maple syrup are not interchangeable, and honey is a bit more forgiving regarding the amount used in recipes.

You may have noticed that some maple syrup brands are sweeter than others, which is okay. Make sure you use maple syrup with only one ingredient—maple syrup.

All the granola recipes on the next few pages include a sweetener such as honey or maple syrup, except for one that is sweetened by fruit. This granola tested surprisingly high among my friends. But it is not only for those following a stoic granola philosophy, i.e., granola purists.

As you will discover, cinnamon, nutmeg, or cayenne pepper can change the whole dynamic of granola. Currently, my favorite way to make granola is to use all three.

As far as fillers go, I prefer almonds and pecans, my two favorite nuts. You can mix and match other nuts if you prefer.

All the recipes call for regular oats and not instant oats. I have tested instant oats and found regular oats taste better.

When baking the granola, there are two different granola processes. One involves roasting the oats first, then adding the nuts, mixing the sweeteners and spices, and roasting them together. The second method is to add the sweeteners after roasting the oats and nuts.

This is by no means an Ayurvedic cookbook, but I have some friends that are experts in Ayurvedic medicine, and they say that according to Ayurvedic principles, you should not heat honey. I know what you are thinking—this is a whole new thing to worry about. Relax; you can make great granola without baking with honey, and maple syrup is also a good option.

One expected benefit of adding honey after the oats and nuts are roasted is that you need less. Cooking the honey seems to lessen its strength, so you can make a lower-calorie version of granola by adding it later in the process.

The idea that ingredients mellow as they're cooked must be incredibly obvious for those who cook. Put a bunch of spices in a cold glass of water, and it can be a bit harsh, but if you heat it up and it tastes like soup, that is delicious.

Some more thoughts before you start: You can add 1/4–1/2 cup of coconut to any of the granola recipes. I usually add about 1/4 cup whenever I make granola unless I don't have any coconut in the house; I obviously can't add something I don't have.

You should also know that I always use a raisin paste as a binder. I have tried making a date paste, but to my surprise, I found that the raisin paste tasted better in the granola. I also tried roasting the oats in butter instead of oil, but I didn't get as good of a result.

I could bore you for hours with all the ways I tried to make granola that did not work, and as a result, these concoctions did not make this book.

Thomas Edison once said I have not failed in making a light bulb; I have discovered 10,000 ways not to make a light bulb. He eventually invented the light bulb, but I don't think he ever came up with a good granola recipe, and he died from snack frustration. Luckily, you have this Granola Manifesto to save you from such a horrible fate!

Imagine your favorite song playing in the background while turning this page.

Chewy Classic Granola – Honey Version

Well-rounded granola—I think this should be your first one. It has received great reviews internationally … at least locally … at least with my group of friends. Seriously, this is a classic.

1 cup oats	1/2 tablespoon cinnamon
1/2 cup almonds	1/2 cup raisins
1/2 cup pecans	1/8 to 1/4 cup honey
1 tablespoon coconut oil	1/8 to 1/4 teaspoon salt

Preheat the oven to 300 degrees.

While the oven is preheating, put the almonds and pecans in the food processor, and process them until they are broken into pieces. You may want to process the almonds first, then the pecans, because the almonds require more time in the food processor. If you have a good food processor, this can happen in a few seconds. Put the chopped nuts in a bowl.

So, the recipe calls for 1/8 to 1/4 cup of honey and 1/8 to 1/4 teaspoon of salt. You might wonder, "Now what?" For the honey, pour enough to fill the measuring cup about halfway between the 1/8 to 1/4 cup lines. Add either 1/8 or 1/4 of a teaspoon or somewhere in between for the salt.

Mix the honey, coconut oil, salt, and cinnamon.

Spread the oats in a Pyrex pan, and once the oven is preheated, put the pan of oats in the oven for 10 minutes.

While the oats are baking, put the raisins in the food processor and process them into a paste.

After 10 minutes of baking the oats, open the oven and add the chopped pecans and almonds. Bake for another 10 minutes.

Once the nuts and oats are done baking, remove the pan from the oven.

Add the honey mixture to the oats and nuts in the pan and stir until completely covered.

(To my Ayurvedic friends, if you are concerned about the honey getting too hot, let the pan sit for a minute or two, then add the honey mixture, but don't wait too long because the oats and nuts need to be at least very warm.)

Next, make a pile of oats and nuts and fold the raisin paste into the oat and nuts; push on the mixture with the back of a spoon and slide across the pan, applying pressure on the mix. Once the raisin paste is completely incorporated into the oat and nut mix, shape the mixture into a block about 1 inch thick.

Now push down on the granola from the top and then push it from the side to get rid of the air pockets.

You may have to use a clean spoon when shaping the granola into a block. Also, you can use a spatula and press down on top of the granola. Then push the side edge of the granola with the spatula as well.

Once condensed into a block, let it cool for about 30 minutes. Then you can cut out a piece with a knife.

Congratulations, you have made granola from scratch. You know what is in it and how it was processed; you know it inside and out. Good job!

Now you can walk around with an air of superiority because you know how to make chewy granola bars. Start treating everyone else like buffoons and speak only in the third person.

Chewy Classic Granola—Maple Syrup

This is very similar to the previous recipe, except it uses Maple Syrup.

1 cup oats	1/2 tablespoon cinnamon
1/2 cup almonds	1/2 cup raisins
1/2 cup pecans	3 tablespoons maple syrup
1 tablespoon coconut oil	1/8 to 1/4 teaspoon salt

Preheat the oven to 300 degrees.

While the oven is preheating, put the almonds and pecans in the food processor and process them until they are broken into pieces. You may want to process the almonds before the pecans because almonds require more time in the food processor. If you have a good food processor, this can happen in a few seconds. Put the chopped nuts in a bowl.

So, the recipe calls for 1/8 to 1/4 teaspoon of salt, and you might wonder, "Now what?" Either add 1/8 or 1/4 of a teaspoon or somewhere in between—either is fine.

Mix the maple syrup, coconut oil, salt, and cinnamon.

Spread the oats in a Pyrex pan, and once the oven is preheated, put the pan of oats in the oven for 10 minutes.

While the oats are baking, put the raisins in the food processor and process them into a paste.

After 10 minutes of baking the oats, open the oven and take out the Pyrex pan; add the chopped pecans and almonds into the pan. Pour the maple syrup mixture on top of the oats and nuts and be sure to scrape the bottom of the container that held the maple syrup mix so all of the maple syrup and salt goes into the pan of oats and nuts. Mix the oats and nuts so they are covered with the maple syrup mixture. Bake for another 8 minutes.

Once the nuts and oats are done baking, remove the pan from the oven.

Now make a pile of oats and nuts and fold the raisin paste into the oat and nuts; push on the mixture with the back of a spoon and slide across the pan, applying pressure on the mix. Once the raisin paste is completely incorporated into the oat and nut mix, shape the mixture into a block about 1 inch thick.

Now the goal is to push down on the granola from the top and push it from the side to get rid of all the air pockets.

You may have to use a clean spoon when shaping the granola into a block. You can also use a spatula, press down on the granola, and then push on the side edge of the granola.

Once condensed into a block, let it cool for about 30 minutes. Then you can cut out a piece with a knife.

Granola Bar—For the Purist

Make sure you eventually try this one. In blind taste tests, some people prefer this one over others.

1 cup oats	1/2 cup dates
1/2 cup pecans	1/2 cup raisins
1/2 cup almonds	1/8 to 1/4 teaspoon sea salt
1/2 tablespoon cinnamon	

Preheat the oven to 300 degrees.

While the oven is preheating, put the almonds and pecans in the food processor, and process them until they are broken into pieces. You may want to process the almonds first, then the pecans, because almonds require more time in the food processor. If you have a good food processor, this can happen in a few seconds. Put the chopped nuts in a bowl.

Spread out the oats in a Pyrex pan. Once the oven is done preheating, put the pan of oats in the oven.

So, the recipe calls for 1/8 to 1/4 teaspoon of salt, and you might wonder, "Now what?" Add either 1/8 or 1/4 of a teaspoon or somewhere between.

While the oats are baking, put the dates, raisins, cinnamon, and salt in the food processor and process them into a paste.

After 10 minutes of baking the oats, open the oven, and add the chopped pecans and almonds. Bake for another 10 minutes.

Once the nuts and oats are done baking, remove the pan from the oven.

Now make a pile of oats and nuts and fold the date/raisin paste into the oat and nuts; push on the mixture with the back of a spoon and slide across the pan, applying pressure on the mix. Once the date/raisin paste is completely incorporated into the oat and nut mix, shape the mixture into a block about 1 inch thick.

Now the goal is to push down on the granola from the top and push it from the side to get rid of all the air pockets.

You may have to use a clean spoon when shaping the granola into a block. You can use a spatula and press down on top of the granola. Then push the side edge of the granola with the spatula as well.

I had a conversation with the Universe, and it was interesting.

Nutmeg Chewy Granola

This is also a good, well-rounded granola. The nutmeg really changes the flavor.

1 cup oats	1/8 to 1/4 cup honey
1/2 cup almonds	1 tablespoon coconut oil
1/2 cup pecans	1/4–1/2 teaspoon sea salt
1/2 cup raisins	1/2 tablespoon cinnamon
1/2 teaspoon nutmeg	

Preheat the oven to 300 degrees.

While the oven is preheating, put the almonds and pecans in the food processor and process them until they are broken into pieces. You may want to process the almonds before the pecans because almonds take more time in the food processor.

If you have a good food processor, this can happen in a few seconds. Put the chopped nuts in a bowl.

So, the recipe calls for 1/8 to 1/4 of a cup of honey and 1/8 to 1/4 teaspoon of salt. You might wonder, "Now what?" Pour the honey about halfway between the 1/8 to 1/4 cup lines in the measuring cup. For the salt, add 1/8 to 1/4 of a teaspoon.

Mix the honey, coconut oil, salt, nutmeg, and cinnamon.

Spread the oats in a Pyrex pan. Once the oven is preheated, put the pan of oats in the oven for 10 minutes.

While the oats are baking, put the raisins in the food processor and process them into a paste.

After 10 minutes of baking the oats, open the oven and add the chopped pecans and almonds. Bake for another 10 minutes.

Once the nuts and oats are done baking, remove the pan from the oven.

Add the honey mixture to the oats and nuts in the pan and stir until completely covered.

(To my Ayurvedic friends, if you are concerned about the honey getting too hot, let the pan sit for a minute or two, then add the honey mixture. Don't wait too long because the oats and nuts need to at least be very warm.)

Now make a pile of oats and nuts and fold the raisin paste into the oat and nut mix; push on the mixture with the back of a spoon and slide across the pan, applying pressure on the mix. Once the raisin paste is completely incorporated into the oat and nut mix, shape the mixture into a block about 1 inch thick.

Push down on the granola from the top and side to get rid of all the air pockets.

You may have to use a clean spoon when shaping the granola into a block. You can also use a spatula and press down on top of the granola. Then push the side edge of the granola with the spatula.

Once condensed into a block, let it cool for about 30 minutes. Then you can cut out a piece with a knife.

You may think, "This recipe is the same as the classic granola recipe, but with nutmeg." That is true, but snack understanding unfolds one step at a time.

Rogers and Hammerstein did not compose the music for *The Sound of Music* the first day they learned to play an instrument; they did other things first. We know what Rogers and Hammerstein did not do; they did not make amazing granola bars because they did not have this recipe. Imagine how good *The Sound of Music* might have been if they had eaten a granola bar with nutmeg.

Chewy Granola—Hot and Spicy Granola

This granola has a more complex and robust flavor, but I'm not sure if kids will like it or if they should eat it because of the cayenne pepper. I have found that 3–4 big shakes are what most people like.

1 cup oats	1/8 to 1/4 cup honey
1/2 cup almonds	1 tablespoon coconut oil
1/2 cup pecans	1/8 to 1/4 teaspoon sea salt
1/2 cup raisins	1/2 teaspoon cinnamon
1/2 teaspoon nutmeg	
3 or 4 big shakes of cayenne pepper	

Preheat the oven to 300 degrees.

While the oven is preheating, put the almonds and pecans in the food processor and process them until they are broken into pieces. You may want to process the almonds before the pecans because the almonds require more time in the food processor. If you have a good food processor, this can happen in a few seconds. Put the chopped nuts in a bowl.

So, the recipe calls for 1/8 to 1/4 of a cup of honey and 1/8 to 1/4 teaspoon of salt; you might wonder, "Now what?" Pour the honey about halfway between the 1/8 to 1/4 cup lines in the measuring cup. Add between 1/8 or 1/4 of a teaspoon of salt.

Mix the honey, coconut oil, salt, cinnamon, nutmeg, and cayenne pepper.

Spread the oats in a Pyrex pan. Once the oven is preheated, put the pan of oats in the oven for 10 minutes.

While the oats are baking, put the raisins in the food processor and process them into a paste.

After 10 minutes of baking the oats, open the oven and add the chopped pecans and almonds. Bake for another 10 minutes.

Once the nuts and oats are done baking, remove the pan from the oven.

Add the honey mixture to the oats and nuts in the pan and stir until completely covered.

(To my Ayurvedic friends, if you are concerned about the honey getting too hot, let the pan sit for a minute or two, then add the honey mixture, but don't wait too long because the oats and nuts need to at least be very warm.)

Now make a pile of oats and nuts and fold the raisin paste into the oat and nuts; push on the mixture with the back of a spoon and slide across the pan, applying pressure on the mix. Once the raisin paste is completely incorporated into the oat and nut mix, shape the mixture into a block about 1 inch thick.

Push down on the granola from the top and side to get rid of all the air pockets.

You may have to use a clean spoon when shaping the granola into a block. Also, you can use a spatula and press down on top of the granola. Then push the side edge of the granola with the spatula.

Once condensed into a block, let it cool for about 30 minutes. Then you can cut a piece with a knife.

Deep thoughts. Not now. I am too busy enjoying granola.

Loose Granola—Spicy

I really like this one. I eat it as cereal with almond milk and a topping for other stuff. After everything is cooked, add raisins, dried apples, and other dried fruit if you like. Believe in your granola intuition, and you will be fine.

1 cup oats	1 tablespoon coconut oil
1/2 cup almonds	1/4-1/2 teaspoon sea salt
1/2 cup pecans	1/2 tablespoon cinnamon
3 tablespoons maple syrup	1/2 teaspoon nutmeg
3 or 4 big shakes of cayenne pepper (optional)	

Preheat the oven to 300 degrees.

While the oven is preheating, put the almonds and pecans into the food processor and process until they are broken into pieces. You may want to process the almonds before the pecans because almonds take more time in the food processor. If you have a good food processor, this can happen in a few seconds. Put the chopped nuts in a bowl.

So, the recipe calls for 1/8 to 1/4 teaspoon of salt, and you might wonder, "Now what?" Add between 1/8 or 1/4 of a teaspoon of salt.

Mix the maple syrup, coconut oil, salt, cinnamon, nutmeg, and cayenne pepper. Spread out the oats in a Pyrex pan. Spread the oats in a Pyrex pan, and once the oven is preheated, put the pan of oats in the oven for 10 minutes.

After 10 minutes of baking the oats, open the oven, take out the Pyrex pan, and add the chopped pecans and almonds into the pan. Pour the maple syrup mixture on top of the oats and nuts and be sure to scrape the bottom of the container that held the maple syrup mix so all the maple syrup and spices go into the pan of oats and nuts.

Mix the oats and nuts so they are covered with the maple syrup mixture. Bake for another 8 minutes.

Once the nuts and oats are done baking, remove the pan from the oven.

While the granola is hot, stir it around, and loosen it up from the bottom of t the pan. Let it cool and store it in a sealed container. The container has to be sealed, or the granola will get limp.

No oven is the same, so if you don't think the granola is crispy enough, try baking it a little longer. You can also put it back in after it is done for a refresh.

I am only your granola guide, and I can only take you so far. You may want to add less of ingredients or a bit more. Believe in your granola intuition, and you will be fine—Deja Vous.

Movements and shifts

You may have experienced a granola paradigm shift. It happens, and when it does—embrace it.

This is the end of the granola section of the cookbook, in case you were wondering, "When will this end?"

The Random Recipe Section

I have not read "Hamlet" or "War and Peace" but I don't think they have a "Random Recipe Section". However, don't let that get you down because the literary work that you are currently engaged in has filled this void. Welcome to the Random Recipe Section!

I hope you enjoy this assortment of random recipes.

Sweet Potato Crepes

Every couple of weeks, I will cook four or five sweet potatoes. I will then peel the potatoes and put the peeled, cooked potatoes in a covered bowl or plastic container to eat over the next day or two.

It bothered me that I was not eating the skins. So, while the oven is still hot, here is a way to use the skin well. Technically, it is not a crepe, but I don't think many people will know the difference.

1 banana	1/2 lemon
4 sweet potatoes	Some raisins (optional)
Some pecans (optional)	

Preheat the oven to 350 degrees.

Wash the potatoes thoroughly, then bake for about an hour. While the potatoes are baking, completely mash the banana in a bowl, squeeze half a lemon, and thoroughly mix. Optional—Add a few raisins and some chopped-up pecans.

When done baking, take sweet potatoes out of the oven and scoop out the potato until you are left with just the skin. Flatten the skin out and cut into approximately 2-inch-wide strips. Scoop the banana mix onto the sweet potato skins. Roll up the potato skins like you are rolling a cigar. Just don't try to smoke it.

Bake for 20 minutes.

Tastes great hot.

Potato Slices

A confession—I love ketchup, But this is not a ketchup book. This is a snack book. Don't worry; the ketchup comment will make sense in a moment.

2 potatoes

half of an avocado

1/4 teaspoon of salt (or less)

Preheat the oven to 375.

Mash up avocado (best if the avocado is really ripe), add salt and stir together.

Slice potatoes into wedges the size of steak fries or French fries you would get at a nice restaurant.

Put the avocado/salt mix in a plastic bag with the potato wedges and move the wedges around, so they are coated with avocado.

Bake for one hour.

I eat with ketchup.

Advanced Intermediate: Can add about 10 shakes of cayenne pepper to the avocado mixture for extra spiciness.

Tea Party Dessert Soup

Great at parties, and make sure you make enough. Everyone will want seconds.

16 strawberries

slice of watermelon without pits—
put twice as much watermelon as
strawberries.

2 or 3 spoonfuls of applesauce—
optional if you don't have it, don't
worry about it.

Put strawberries and watermelon in a food processor. Then add the applesauce.
Pour into a bowl.

Add walnuts to the mixture and serve chilled.

Energize Me Now

This seemed weird to me too. However, for whatever reason, I really like this snack. This is great to eat for lunch or brunch. It often gives me a blast of energy. I feel like all the ingredients compete for my attention when I eat this.

1/2 avocado	pepper
1 teaspoon of apple cider vinegar	3 big shakes of cayenne
1/2 cup carrots or (about 8 baby carrots)	3 dates

Mash avocado really well and add the apple cider vinegar and cayenne pepper. Finely chop the carrots and dates into chunks and add them to the avocado mix.

If using a food processor, put avocado in the food processor and blend until creamy, then add the rest of the ingredients and blend until gravel-like consistency.

Blast off into the rest of the day.

Carrot Salad and Avocado

I have to tell you; this is good stuff.

1/8 cup raisins

1 teaspoon apple cider vinegar

1/2 cup carrots
(about 8 baby carrots)

1/2 small spoonful of brown
mustard

1/8 avocado

Dash of salt

Dash of pepper

Shred carrots in a food processor or manually chop them into a coleslaw-like consistency. Mix apple cider vinegar, brown mustard, and salt and pepper in a bowl. Add shredded carrot and raisins to the brown mustard mix and stir together.

Finally, a Bacon Free Broccoli Salad

1 1/2 cups chopped broccoli	1/4 cup onion
1/8 cup raisins	1/4 cup pineapple
1/2 avocado	1 tablespoon honey
3 tablespoons of balsamic vinegar	

Chop broccoli and pineapple into relatively small pieces (about dime size) and finely chop the onion.

Mix broccoli, onions, raisins, pineapple, honey, and balsamic vinegar in a bowl. Really mix the ingredients so that the tops of the broccoli get covered in balsamic vinegar.

In another small bowl, mash up the avocado. Add the avocado to the broccoli so that the balsamic vinegar and avocado cover all the broccoli. Stir in raisins and let this sit overnight in the refrigerator.

Hot Nuts

I plead the fifth and will not make a ridiculous comment here.

1/2 cup pecans	1/2 cup almonds
1/4 cup raisins	1 teaspoon spoonful of honey
3 or 4 shakes of cinnamon	3 or 4 shakes of cayenne pepper
Dash of sea salt (to taste)	

Put honey in a pot or bowl—I use a pot, making it easier to stir. Add sea salt, cayenne pepper, and cinnamon; stir everything together. Add all nuts and stir, so nuts are coated with honey mixture. Add raisins and mix together gently.

The short version of the directions—mix everything together, then eat it

Hot Nuts—Ginger Variation

1 cup pecans	1 cup almonds
1 cup walnuts	1 cup raisins
4 tablespoons honey	1/4 teaspoon cinnamon
3 tablespoons apple juice	1/4 teaspoon sea salt
1 tablespoon ginger paste	3 dates

Process the dates, ginger, and apple juice in the food processor until the mixture is the consistency of a paste. Put all the nuts in a bowl and stir in the ginger paste until all the nuts are covered. Add the rest of the ingredients and gently stir.

Cashew Bars

You can also eat these raw

1 cup cashews	1 teaspoon honey
4 small dates or 2 really big dates	dash of sea salt

Preheat the oven to 350 degrees.

Put cashews in a food processor and pulverize them into a sand-like texture. Then add the dates, honey, and sea salt to the food processor and pulverize—shape the mixture into bars a little less than 1/2 an inch thick. Place on Pyrex pan, bake for seven minutes, then flip. Bake for five minutes, then remove from oven.

Hot Banana

Warning: Just heat the mashed banana until it gets warm and remove it before it gets hot; if the banana gets really hot, the texture gets really weird. Another tip, you can bake a banana, but I think it tastes better to mash it up and cook it on the stovetop. Reminds me of that old saying Stove top mashed banana instead of potatoes.

1 banana   1/8 of a cup of raisins—optional

2 or 3 shakes of cinnamon

Mash up the banana and put it in a pot. Heat at medium-low heat. Add cinnamon to taste — I add about 5 shakes.

For advanced personnel—add some raisins and pecans or almonds
Optional—can add a little apple juice (actually, everything is optional)

Hot Banana Soup

Bonus observation: For some reason, when you add cinnamon to hot apple juice, it makes it taste like hot apple cider. Isn't that interesting?

1 banana	1 cup of apple juice
4 Shakes of cinnamon or to taste—I usually put 4 big shakes	1/4 cup of raisins—optional, but I usually add them

Put cinnamon and apple juice in a pot. Cut banana into bite-sized pieces and add to the pot.

Cover on low heat, stirring occasionally. Heat until it starts to get really warm.

Banana Revenge—for mature audiences

A banana by itself can be boring, but with nuts and cayenne pepper, it changes everything. This one is pretty high on the list of the hierarchy of snacks.

1 banana	1/8 cup almonds
1/8 cup raisins	One or two, or three shakes of cayenne pepper

Add almonds and banana to the food processor and process for about 20 to 30 seconds or until almonds are about gravel size.

Add raisins and shake in one or two or three shakes of cayenne pepper and stir. If this is your first time, try just one shake. I usually put in two shakes.

This is a borderline Fruit and Nut Fun Bowl recipe, but this is more or less the banana section. Feel free to tear out this page and staple it into the Fruit and Nut Fun Bowl section—either way, things will be okay.

Ice Cream Alternatives Section

I call these ice cream alternatives because I eat this stuff around the same time you might eat ice cream. This section includes one too many brown rice-based recipes as well.

Coconut yogurt and Nuts

Don't take the simplicity of this for granted. Some people like this more than ice cream. So,this is a reminder that this is a nice alternative to ice cream.

1 cup plain coconut yogurt

1/8 cup raisins

1/4 cup walnuts

1/8 cup almonds

1 or 2 tablespoons of honey

Mix all ingredients together.

You can either shake cinnamon on top or mix into the yogurt

Really, you call that a recipe – mix nuts into yogurt. Wow, what a revolutionary concept. What's next?

Bonus Recipe – Apple

1 apple

Pick up an apple and bite

About as groundbreaking as the Coconut yogurt and Nuts recipe.

Okay, okay, just remember The Granola Code section.

Banana Coconut yogurt and Nuts

1 whole or half overripe banana	1/2 cup plain coconut yogurt
1/8 cup almonds	1/8 cup pecans
1/8 cup raisins	1/2-1 teaspoon of honey

Completely mash-up either a whole or half a banana. It does not have to be overripe, but I find that overripe bananas are sweeter. Mash until it is like soft glue.

How much banana you use and the sweetness of the banana determines how much honey you add.

Add the coconut yogurt and mix it together. Add the rest of the ingredients. You can either shake cinnamon on top or mix it into the coconut yogurt.

Brown Rice Pudding

Dairy Free but still thick, this is a great way to trick people into thinking that there is cream in this when there is none.

1 cup cooked brown rice	1 cup almond or regular milk
1/2 to whole tablespoon honey	1/8 cup raisins
3 to 4 big shakes of cinnamon	2 1/2 teaspoons oats (preferably instant but can use regular oats)

Put oats in the food processor and blend into a powder—basically, you make oat flour.

Put almond milk in a pot and heat at medium-low heat, and stir in oat flour. If it is instant oatmeal, it will get thicker in about three or four minutes. Regular oatmeal will take closer to six to eight minutes to thicken. Once thick, stir in the honey, then add the brown rice raisins. Sprinkle cinnamon on top.

I really like this, and thickening the almond milk makes it seem creamier.

Brown Rice Banana Pudding

Optional: If it tastes too thick, you may need to add a few splashes of almond milk. I usually think it is fine, but it depends on how ripe the banana is. It is called a snack, but it is pretty good for breakfast.

1 banana	1 cup brown rice
1/4 cup raisins (optional)	few dashes of cinnamon (optional)

Mash up the banana completely. Add brown rice and stir. Stop here and try it. I like it just like this.

But it is also great with raisins and cinnamon.

Rice Pudding—Alternative Method

Well, personally, I love this. But then again, I am biased.

1 cup cooked rice	1/2 cup coconut milk
1/8 cup raisins	4 drops of vanilla
1/2 slightly overripe banana dash of cinnamon	1-2 teaspoons of honey (if you buy unsweetened coconut milk)

Mash up the banana completely and mix it with coconut milk until it becomes a thick liquid. Then add rice, raisins, cinnamon, and vanilla and stir together.

Sometimes I don't know what I am doing at the supermarket, so I pick up sweetened coconut milk or almond milk. If you do the same, don't worry about it; just don't add any additional honey. However, if you get unsweetened coconut milk, add one or two teaspoons of honey.
Actually, add just one spoon, then test it—sweeten to how you like it.

I usually like a lot of cinnamon, but for this, I go on the lighter side.

Strawberry Brown Rice Pudding

I think that 2 tablespoons of honey make it too sweet. I almost always add six strawberries mainly because I can't come up with a good reason I shouldn't.

4-6 medium-sized strawberries

1 tablespoon honey

1 cup brown rice
(already cooked)

1/2 cup plain nonfat
coconut yogurt

Mix honey and coconut yogurt together and add brown rice and mix together. Cut up strawberries and add to mix.

Cheesecake Substitute and Coconut yogurt substitute

Over Analysis

The sweetness of the banana makes a big difference in this snack. If you are some type of purist, you can use unsweetened almond milk and just add 4 or 5 dates and no honey. It will come out pretty sweet as well.

1 banana	1/4 cup of almond milk
8 shakes of cinnamon	optional: add almonds, pecans, raisins
1 cup of brown rice (already cooked)	1 teaspoon of honey—if using unsweetened almond milk, add 1/2 teaspoon cap of vanilla

Put brown rice, banana, almond milk, vanilla, almonds, and honey (if using unsweetened almond milk) in the food processor and blend for a few minutes, occasionally scraping down the sides

If it is too thick for your liking, add a little more almond milk, which I always do. I try and get the consistency of coconut yogurt.

After blended, you can add nuts like Pecans and Raisins

Sweetness—if you like it sweeter can add a little more honey. If it is too sweet, use unsweetened almond milk

Bean Cooking

Sure, you could buy garbanzo beans (chickpeas) out of a can, but I always feel better when I cook the dried beans from the package. Why? Because then I know what the beans have been cooked in.

Cooking beans is easy; once you have them on hand, you can live an on-the-go lifestyle. I like to cook a couple of cups of beans at the beginning of the week and then scoop out a cup whenever I am hungry.

You can either soak the beans first or just put them in a pot and cook them. I always prefer soaking the beans; I have heard that soaking makes them easier to digest. It also significantly reduces the cooking time. Garbanzo beans typically come in 14-ounce or 16-ounce bags; you can use these cooking instructions for either size.

The no-soak method (not recommended)

First, rinse the beans, put them in a big pot, and add 8 cups water. Bring the water to a boil, then turn down to medium-low heat and cover the pot—Cook for another 2 ½ hours. Try one or two of the beans; keep cooking until they are soft.

Soaking method

Rinse the beans; place them in a large bowl and add 6 cups of water. I usually cover the beans and put them in the refrigerator at this stage; however, I have been told that you can leave them on the counter.

Allow the beans to soak overnight or all day. When they are done soaking, drain the water and put them into a big pot with 6 cups of fresh water. Bring to a boil, then cover and lower the heat. Cook until soft, about 30 to 60 minutes.

Bean FAQs (fascinating answers to questions)

Q: I forgot to cook the beans after they soaked; now what?

A: First, try not to panic, although it is understandable if you do. When you stop sweating, take a little plastic wrap, cover the beans, and put them in the refrigerator. Write "Cook beans" (don't forget the quotation marks) on a piece of paper. Put the note somewhere you will see it, and make sure to cook the beans within the next 8 hours.

Q: Don't you lose nutrients when you throw out the soaking water?

A: You are not losing many nutrients because the beans are drawing water in, and most nutrients remain in the beans. More or less a made-up answer, but it might be more or less true.

Q: So, what else is new?

A: Not much.

Garbanzo Beans (Chickpeas) Mediterranean

Snack Warning: If you try to eat this before you heat it, the onion and garlic will be a bit harsh. Be sure to heat it first, then eat. Once cooked, it is really pretty good hot or cold.

1 cup chickpeas (canned or pre-cooked)	Dash of salt
14 shakes curry powder	Dash of pepper
1 garlic clove	2 big spoonfuls of olive oil
1/8 of a big onion or 1/4 of a medium onion	

Mash up the chickpeas. Finely chop the onion and garlic, then add to the mashed chickpeas along with the olive oil, curry, salt, and pepper.
Mix thoroughly. Alternatively, you can add all ingredients to a food processor and blend them into a paste. Add the bean mixture into a pot; heat and stir for a few minutes until warm-to-hot. Turn off the stove and let it sit there for about 3 minutes. Now it is ready to eat.

Final Thoughts

If you find even just a few new snack recipes that you cook for the rest of your life, then I would consider this book a big success. Thank you, and don't stress out about any of this stuff; it is only snack food.

I now know how John Steinbeck felt when he wrote *Grapes of Wrath*. Writing a book is a pretty major undertaking, even if it is a cookbook.

"May you find inner peace, a healthy outlook, and snack perfection."

~Stan Starsky
Really good-selling author (not the best but pretty good)

************* National Snack Certificate*************

have successfully completed three great snacks, and I feel great about it.

Congratulations _____.

Certificate of Completion date

Great job! You are well on your way to inner peace, a healthy outlook, and snack perfection.

Personally awarded to you by Stan Starsky.

************* Quiz At The End Of This Book*************

What is the ideal degree and time sequence for roasting oats and nuts for granola?

I am thinking of a number; what number am I thinking of?

Name two company names that sound just as silly as the term "Fruit and Nut Fun Bowl".

How many dips does it take to fall in love with this dip
(hint the title of this dip will give it away)?

Is it possible to make a broccoli salad without using bacon and mayonnaise?

What is your favorite snack from this book?
(there is no wrong answer for this one)